HOW TO BE
PRESENT

Embrace the Art of Mindfulness to Discover
Peace and Joy Every Day

Sophie Golding

HOW TO BE PRESENT

Text by Sibylla Nash

Published in the United States by Viva Editions, an imprint of Start Midnight, LLC, 221 River Street, Ninth Floor, Hoboken, New Jersey 07030

Trade Paper ISBN: 978-1-63228-086-2

E-book ISBN: 978-1-63228-143-2

CONTENTS

INTRODUCTION

If you've found your way to this book, perhaps it's
because you're searching for something. Maybe
you're looking to experience more of what life has
to offer. You want to feel the wind at your back
and the sun on your face, and understand what
it means to be human. We have the capacity to
laugh and to cry to express our joys and sorrows,
and when we are present in the moment, we can
fully experience and appreciate these emotions.

By living in the present, we're able to truly
appreciate the wonder of simply being alive.
Come on this journey as we explore ways
to make the most of each moment.

CHAPTER ONE

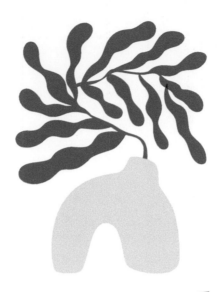

THE ART OF BEING PRESENT

When you live in the present, you become engaged in the here and now. You learn to be aware of your feelings, your body and your surroundings in the moment. Studies have shown that living in the present moment can reduce anxiety and give you a better sense of well-being. This is because when you stop worrying about what's coming you no longer miss out on the joy of the here and now. The now can be full of beauty and wonder, and it's yours to experience. Read on to discover how to practice being present in your daily life.

The only thing that is ultimately real about your journey is the step that you're taking at this moment. That's all there ever is.

Eckhart Tolle

PRACTICE
MINDFULNESS

Mindfulness is about maintaining an awareness of your thoughts and feelings without any judgement, and allows you to be fully immersed in the moment. The many benefits of mindfulness are well documented and include reducing anxiety, training your brain to focus and improving your mood. You can start by paying attention to your world and your feelings. Instead of rushing through your actions, slow down and be deliberate. Be aware of your surroundings and notice how each of your senses is engaged. Being mindful is the first step to learning how to be present in your daily life.

All that is important is this
one moment in movement.
Make the moment important,
vital, and worth living.
Do not let it slip away
unnoticed and unused.

Martha Graham

START YOUR DAY WITH INTENTION

Before you begin your day, while you're still in bed, take a few deep breaths and notice the sensations as you inhale and exhale. Perhaps place your hands on your abdomen and feel it rise and fall with each breath. Let yourself fully awaken, but don't rush; the day will still be there. Be aware of how you feel in that moment, then set an intention for how you would like to feel for the rest of the day.

An intention can be something as simple as, "I will feel peace throughout the day," or, "I choose to see the positive in every situation." You may want to write it down so you can look at it throughout the day.

Life will inevitably throw curveballs at you. Maybe someone will show up late to a meeting, or you'll get cut off in traffic. Use your intention to guide you to stay in the present moment. Instead of reacting, slowly inhale and exhale before saying your intention – just once or several times.

TREAT EACH DAY LIKE A FRESH START

Every morning when you wake up, you have the opportunity start over. It's a brand new day! Go into it with awe and wonder. Don't base your expectations on what happened yesterday or last week, and don't worry about what may happen next week.

Instead, realize that today is full of possibilities, all waiting for you. You can't change the past and you can't control the future, but you can focus on what's in front of you now – today!

The secret of health for both mind and body is not to mourn for the past, worry about the future, or anticipate troubles, but to live the present moment wisely and earnestly.

Bukkyō Dendō Kyokai

LIMIT YOUR DISTRACTIONS

You may miss out on the joys of life because you're too busy checking your phone or updating your status on social media. Give yourself some breathing room. Try turning off your phone or at least silencing your notifications for a short period each day – aim for 30 minutes to an hour. By limiting your distractions, you're able to keep your attention on the moment at hand.

Wherever you are —
be all there.

Jim Elliot

REPEAT A POSITIVE MANTRA

If you're feeling stressed or you want to calm your mind, find a saying that resonates with you that can be spoken out loud or repeated silently. It can be a single word, like *shanti*, which means "peace" in Sanskrit, a single note like "om" (a sacred Hindu mantra) or a phrase that is also an affirmation, for example: "I am grateful for this moment." Use it to calm your mind and bring you back to the present. Studies have shown that chanting a mantra lowers your heart rate and decreases your anxiety.

I am here

SLOW DOWN

We live in a fast-paced world. It can be easy to rush through activities with friends and family, never fully appreciating the time we spend with them because we have somewhere else to be or something else to do. Before we know it, the day is over and we're already thinking about all the things we haven't done but need to do.

Take your time to savor whatever it is you're doing, big and small. Whether you are sharing a meal with a loved one or visiting a new city for the first time, know that you are exactly where you're supposed to be. Don't think about what comes next or what happened in the past. Consciously slow down and fully engage in what you're doing so you can be mindful of the moment.

Life is just a series of moments. If you focus on them while they are happening, you stay in the present.

I always give myself
Sundays as a spiritual
base of renewal – a day
when I do absolutely
nothing.

I sit in my jammies or take a walk, and I allow myself time to BE - capital B-E - with myself.

Oprah Winfrey

REFRAME YOUR PERCEPTION

You have the power to choose how to feel about the moment you're in. Standing in line at the supermarket or sitting in traffic, you may feel frustrated and impatient. All the waiting makes you want to hurry life along just to get to the next step.

It doesn't have to be that way. You don't have to look at it as waiting for something. Instead, take a deep breath and be aware of your environment and your thoughts. Let go of your frustration and decide to be fully present and enjoy the moment for whatever it brings.

The best gift we can have is living in the present moment and really enjoying it for what it is.

Amy Smart

JUST LISTEN

When you're talking with a friend or co-worker, have you ever been so busy trying to think of how you're going to respond that you totally miss out on what they're saying? Next time, try being fully present by giving the conversation your complete attention and curiosity. The person speaking will truly appreciate it, and you may find that you connect with them on a much deeper level.

EMBRACE YOUR EMOTIONS

Let's face it, emotions can be big and overwhelming at times, which can be inconvenient! You may be in the habit of telling yourself you shouldn't feel or express certain emotions. Your inner dialogue may tell you to stop crying or to pull yourself together, but in practice it can make you feel even worse when you don't acknowledge your feelings, instead keeping them bottled in.

When you live in the present, you feel how you feel without any judgment. So, try this: don't avoid your emotions. Instead, simply observe them as you would any other sensation. Then, to help you stay in the present moment, say aloud how you're feeling. You could also name your emotions and say, "I feel angry," or "I feel jealous."

Learn how to accept your feelings as part of the moment you're in. They don't define you. Allow yourself to feel them and move on.

AVOID AUTOPILOT

Sometimes you may be so used to doing tasks, like preparing school lunches for the kids or washing dishes, you complete them without giving them much thought. It's routine, so you turn on autopilot and get it done.

If you want to live in the present, be aware of what you're doing, even the seemingly mundane things. Take note of your actions and your surroundings. Give the task at hand your full attention.

Look past your thoughts,
so you may drink the pure
nectar of this moment.

Rumi

GIVE YOURSELF A BREAK

Who *hasn't* said there aren't enough hours in the day? You probably have a lot of responsibilities on your plate trying to balance home, work and a social life. No matter how busy your days, try to pause between each task. Whether you stop for a few deep breaths or to enjoy a glass of water, give yourself a chance to regroup and put the previous task behind you before you start a new one. This way, you can give your full attention to the next item on your to-do list.

I choose to constantly increase my awareness of being in the present

DON'T MULTITASK

As you search for that twenty-fifth hour in the day, you may believe that it's more productive to juggle multiple tasks at once. You might think you can achieve twice as much in half the time, but it's debatable how well things get done when you're multitasking. In fact, studies show that when you multitask, your productivity actually drops by as much as 40 percent! Instead of multitasking, try doing just one thing at a time and give it your full attention. Be aware of how it feels when you're fully engaged. When you slow down and do things one at a time, you're no longer wasting the energy it takes for your brain to switch gears. You'll find that you'll be more productive and efficient, and thus more likely to enjoy the task at hand. Living in the moment allows you to focus on one undertaking at a time.

I am grateful
for this moment,
because this moment
is all that I have,
and it is enough

IT'S OKAY NOT TO KNOW ALL THE ANSWERS

Have you ever had a problem that kept you awake at night or poked away at you while you tried to enjoy an activity? As humans, we sometimes have a burning need to fix our problems. When we don't have the answers or solutions, we start to doubt ourselves.

As you strive to live in the present, you'll learn to accept that you may not have all the answers at the moment, and that's okay. You may have to sit with your worry. Observe your concerns without judgment and then move on. You'll discover the answers when you're meant to.

In this moment, there is plenty of time. In this moment, you are precisely as you should be. In this moment, there is infinite possibility.

Victoria Moran

I accept uncertainty
and know it is
part of life

We spend precious hours fearing the inevitable. It would be wise to use that time adoring our families, cherishing our friends and living our lives.

Maya Angelou

REMIND YOURSELF YOU'RE IN THE DRIVER'S SEAT

Some days, it can feel like the world is out of control and nothing seems to be going your way. On those days, you feel like there's nothing you can do. You just need to remember, you've got this. This is your life. When you live in the present, you accept the moment for what it is. Be aware of your emotions and sensations without judgment. Let those feelings come in and recede like ocean waves and choose to move on to the next moment with a positive attitude. While you can't control the moment, you can control your reaction to it, and that is enough.

I accept what each moment brings

NOTICE THE
SENSATIONS

How often do you stop and notice how things feel? Not your emotions, but what your *body* feels? Think about the way the warm mist of rain on a summer's day dances on your skin, or how your favorite sweatshirt feels like a soft hug. Your body lives in the present, and sensations elicit an immediate reaction from your body. Your body can't feel a past or future sensation – it can only detect what's happening now.

Next time your mind starts to wander, or you're worried about something that happened earlier in the day and you want to anchor yourself in the present, find a sensation to focus on. Run your fingers through your hair, touch a tree trunk or notice how your clothes feel against your skin. Focusing your awareness on how something feels will help reconnect you to your body to experience the present moment.

There is only one time that is important – Now! It is the most important time because it is the only time when we have any power.

Leo Tolstoy

RELISH YOUR RITUALS

Do you have a morning routine? Maybe you like to grab a cup of coffee from a certain cafe every day before you start work. Or maybe you have a nightly beauty regimen that you follow religiously. Start to look at these routines as rituals: activities with a sense of purpose. Whatever ritual brings you joy, lean into the moment. Allow yourself plenty of time and, if possible, block out any distractions so you can focus on completing your ritual while being fully present.

I will feel my feelings
no matter what they may be

TAKE NOTE OF YOUR WINS

Always try to recognize and celebrate your wins, no matter how small you feel they are. There are many things worth celebrating every day – you just have to slow down to notice them.

Create a habit of reflecting on your day and highlighting two positive things that happened. By acknowledging these wins, you are training your mind to be more aware of the good within you.

FOCUS ON YOUR STRENGTHS

It's easy to pick on our weaknesses, those parts of ourselves that we can't help but obsess over and wish we could change. Something goes wrong at work, or your friend doesn't text you back and you believe it's all your fault... if only you were better at [you fill in the blank].

While it's healthy to acknowledge your weaknesses, focusing on them prevents you from fully living in the present. Instead, you should celebrate your strengths and concentrate on what you do best.

When you're present for the successes in your life, big and small, you develop an awareness of who you are now, not who you should or could be. You can use that awareness to discover and nurture the positive potential within you. Love yourself for all that you have to offer. You're amazing! When you focus on your strengths, you'll use them more and that means you'll get even better.

ENJOY THE JOURNEY

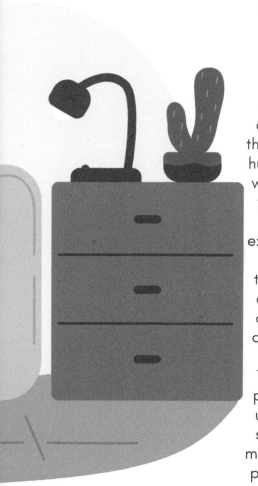

Living in the moment means focusing on the here and now, but this doesn't mean that you shouldn't plan for the future. On the contrary, it's good to dream and have goals. It doesn't matter if your goals include scaling a mountainside or organizing your closet, so long as you have something that you look forward to – that's what dreams are for.

As you go along the path of achieving, don't rush through the process because you're in a hurry to get to your "future life" where you've already reached your goals. You'll miss out on opportunities to grow and explore, and also to be present and fully engaged during those moments. You may also decide to change your goals or dream new dreams. It's all okay and part of your journey.

Take your time and enjoy the process. Your journey is made up of mini destinations. Each step in the process is its own moment of accomplishment: be present for every one of them.

I will be patient
with myself

GET OUT OF
YOUR HEAD

Sometimes you can get in your own way by spending too much time in your head and overthinking things. To be present, you have to let go. Living in the present requires you to be in the moment, to be aware of your surroundings and what's going on around you, and this doesn't leave a lot of time for negative self-talk and self-consciousness.

To live in the present, you have to get out in the world and allow yourself to experience the moment as it happens without any judgment. If you feel negative thoughts getting in the way, replace them with a mantra or breathing exercise.

I let go of the past
so I can move forward

CHAPTER TWO

FREE YOUR MIND

As you practice living in the moment, you may find that sometimes you can't stop your mind from chasing after thoughts and trying to solve problems that haven't happened yet. Maybe this keeps you awake at night or prevents you from fully being present during the day. You realize that your mindset needs to change. A small shift in the way you think can make all the difference. Let's explore ways to help you get rid of any mental barriers that prevent you from living in the moment. Learn the steps you can take to overcome mental blocks that may cause stress and anxiety, and create a habit of being fully present in your life.

CREATE HAPPY THOUGHTS

When you find your stress levels increasing, sometimes all it takes to reduce them is to recall a time when you were happy. Research shows that when you're mindful and all your senses are engaged in an experience, it helps to embed it in your memory, making the recall more vivid. Happy memories can influence your happiness in the present moment.

Next time you're experiencing something that makes you happy, give it your full attention and engage all your senses so you can clearly recall the details later.

If you want to conquer the anxiety of life, live in the moment, live in the breath.

Amit Ray

CHANGE YOUR SELF-TALK

There may be times you wish you were more confident, and the good news is you can be: it all depends on your self-talk. If you're nervous about going to a party because you don't know anyone, instead of zeroing in on the worst-case scenario, change the voice in your head to find the positive.

Don't worry about what could happen; instead, embrace the moment by being fully present and keep your self-talk firmly in the present tense. Say, for example, "I'm having a great time. I'm meeting a lot of interesting people."

Be mindful of your thoughts and accept the power you have to focus on the positive.

I release my anxiety

PRACTICE GRATITUDE

Negative thoughts are inevitable: you're going to have them. To shoo them away, try replacing them with thoughts of gratitude. On those days when you're super stressed and you can't stop your mind from jumping from one worry to the next, center yourself in the moment by taking a calming breath. Start thinking about all you are grateful for in your life at this time. Get a piece of paper, or use an app on your phone, and make a list, big or small; it can include anything from finding a great parking space to being thankful for the loved ones in your life.

You need to remind yourself that things aren't all bad. As you train yourself to pay more attention to the positive, you may find that the goodness in your life starts multiplying as you notice it more.

Studies show that those who practice being thankful experience more optimism and feel better about their lives. So go on, count your blessings!

*Happiness is not
a brilliant climax
to years of grim
struggle and anxiety.*

*It is a long
succession of little
decisions simply
to be happy in
the moment.*

Swami Kriyananda

THOUGHTS CAN BE JUST THOUGHTS

Sometimes you just can't stop your mind from returning to negative thoughts. In those moments, you have to remind yourself they are only thoughts, they're not reality. Your thoughts are not a sign of things to come, and you do not have to act on them. Your thoughts don't control you.

When a negative thought surfaces, try sitting still and take stock of what's happening at that moment. Don't dwell on it, just let it pass freely through your mind and move on.

We're so busy watching out for what's just ahead of us that we don't take time to enjoy where we are.

Bill Watterson

SURROUND YOURSELF WITH POSITIVE PEOPLE

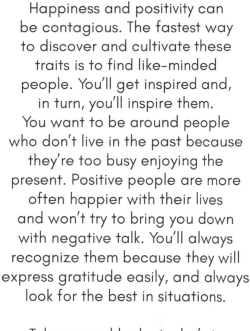

Happiness and positivity can be contagious. The fastest way to discover and cultivate these traits is to find like-minded people. You'll get inspired and, in turn, you'll inspire them. You want to be around people who don't live in the past because they're too busy enjoying the present. Positive people are more often happier with their lives and won't try to bring you down with negative talk. You'll always recognize them because they will express gratitude easily, and always look for the best in situations.

Take a good look at who's in your circle of friends. There's a saying that you're an average of the five people you spend the most time with. If you find that there are some friends who are negative and never have anything positive to say, think about limiting your interactions with them. As you strive to be in the moment and become more aware of your environment, you have the power to choose what type of energy you want to have around you. Decide to surround yourself with the warm and healing vibes of those who only wish the best for you.

GET LOST
IN A BOOK

Have you ever read a book that you just couldn't put down? When it ended, you could feel the presence of characters in the room. Aside from the pleasure you get from being caught up in a page-turner, studies show reading reduces stress and increases empathy. The focus you use while reading is similar to that of meditation, in that you're fully present and engaged in the act; you can't worry about the past or present when you're reading. Try curling up with a good book for at least ten minutes a day.

Anxiety does not
empty tomorrow
of its sorrows, but
only empties today
of its strength.

Charles Spurgeon

LEARN YOUR LESSONS

When you're having trouble letting go of something, be it expectations or a person, do you stop to consider why it's so challenging? As you examine the issue, refrain from judging yourself or the emotions that surface. Just observe.

You go through different experiences in life, and there are teachable moments in those experiences. We can't fully embrace the present until we've let go of the past. Letting go doesn't mean ignoring past experiences; rather, it means taking what you can from the situation, making peace with it however you can and then moving on.

USE SENSORY
DISTRACTIONS

On those days when you're feeling mentally overloaded and you're overcome with stress, try counter-stimulation.

It's a technique used to pull energy away from the event causing you stress. Some people will use white noise. This can be any ambient sound, whether it's the whirring of a fan or radio static. Focus your attention on the sound to redirect your attention and reduce your racing thoughts.

You can also use your other senses for counter-stimulation. Use your sight to focus on an object, essential oils for smell, soak your hands in a sink full of warm or cold water or eat tart foods.

By concentrating fully on one of your senses, you'll pull energy away from any feelings of anxiety you may be experiencing. It's a self-soothing technique that allows you to focus on the present.

I am grateful for the
resources I have available
to me, and I will do
the best I can with
what I have

USE
AFFIRMATIONS

A great way to boost your mood and keep yourself in the present is to use affirmations. Affirmations are positive statements that help you overcome negative thoughts. Over time, if you say them enough, they'll replace your negative beliefs with positive ones.

You can say things like, "I celebrate each moment by being fully present," or, "I accept these feelings, no matter what they are." You can also flip through this book and find a statement that resonates with you. Practice saying it throughout the day.

Tension is who you think you should be. Relaxation is who you are.

Chinese proverb

ALLOW YOURSELF GRACE

Sometimes your expectations can be your own worst enemy: you have an idea in your head about how things are supposed to be, and when they don't turn out that way, you feel like you failed. Maybe you think you're supposed to reach certain milestones by a certain time, or, thanks to social media, you believe you should have a certain lifestyle because everyone else your age seems to have it all. Life may not always work out the way you expect, however, and you are going to make mistakes.

It's okay: go easy on yourself. Give yourself permission not to feel bad when you make a mistake; it happens, and it's not the end of the world. You don't have to be perfect. Instead, show yourself grace in those moments you feel everything is unraveling. Take a deep breath and try not to react. Observe your emotions and don't judge yourself. Repeat to yourself, "I am worthy as I am."

STOP CHASING HAPPINESS

Many people treat happiness as the destination, or the whole point of the journey. "I just want to be happy," they say. Treating happiness as an end goal means you're always living in the future and not giving yourself the opportunity to be fully engaged in the present.

Instead, try shifting your mindset to see happiness like every other emotion – it comes and goes. Then you'll be able to be fully present in your moments without having to worry about labeling the experience or feeling disappointed if it doesn't meet expectations.

I will only focus
on things that
are in my control

OWN YOUR LIFE

Sometimes you can feel bound by expectations. Maybe you feel as though you have to have a job in a particular industry, or a specific look. You may feel under pressure to act or think in accordance with a role you've been cast into by family or friends.

Stop. Take a deep breath. Understand that your life is really yours to do with as you wish. If you want to do something different, do it. Just because you're living a certain way now doesn't mean you have to live that way forever.

When you are fully engaged in the present, you understand that the potential of each day is yours to do with as you please. Next time you feel a sense of pressure to do something, ground yourself in the moment. Take note of your sensations and emotions. Inhale and exhale deeply before asking yourself, what do *you* want to do? Then, go do it.

Anxiety's like a rocking chair.
It gives you something to do,
but it doesn't get you very far.

Jodi Picoult

USE A SENSORY GROUNDING EXERCISE

If you quickly want to center yourself in the present, here is an exercise that encourages you to tune in to your senses – the 5-4-3-2-1 method.

Wherever you are, look around and name five things you can see, four things you can touch, three things you can hear, two things you can smell and one thing you can taste.

This calms your mind by giving it a task to focus on and bringing you into the present moment.

In this moment,
all is well

CHAPTER THREE

BE IN YOUR BODY

We tend to believe our thoughts only reside within our heads, but if you listen to your body, you'll notice that your thoughts are also manifested in physical sensations. Whether it's clammy hands or a dry mouth, these can be reactions to your thoughts. Let's focus on fostering a connection between your mind and body by discovering tips that will help you find joy in movement, healthy eating and understanding what your body and mind are trying to tell you. Because when your mind and body are in harmony, you'll be able to live more fully in the present moment.

I'm letting go of
what doesn't serve me

What the mind dwells upon, the body acts upon.

Denis Waitley

PRACTICE MINDFUL MEDITATION

Meditation can be a wonderful thing to keep in your mental toolbox. Not only does it help to relax your mind, but it grounds you in the present by making you focus on your breathing.

Incorporating mindfulness into your meditation practice will help you develop an intense awareness of how you're feeling and what you're sensing in the moment. Mindfulness meditation doesn't have to be formal - it can be tried anywhere. You can practice it while walking; next time you take a stroll around your neighborhood, walk with awareness. You'll want to take time to observe the sounds, the smells and the sights you encounter on your walk. Do not judge them, just notice them. Your mind may wander, but whenever it does, bring it back by focusing on what you are experiencing and how your body feels as it moves. Be sure to take a moment to pause when you're finished. Exhale and try to bring that awareness to the rest of your day.

STAY HYDRATED

It can be easy to neglect one of our most basic needs: water. Your body needs water to function. Mild dehydration can affect not only your body, but also your mood and your ability to concentrate. Listen to your body and watch out for signs that you need more water, like headaches and low energy.

Try starting your morning with the intention to drink more water throughout the day. You can practice being in the present as you sip your water by paying attention to the sensation of the liquid flowing down your throat. Take a deep breath and exhale between mouthfuls.

A healthy outside

starts from the inside.

Robert Urich

GET UP AND MOVE

Did you know that sometimes all it takes is five to ten minutes of physical activity to boost your mood? Exercise decreases stress hormones and causes feel-good chemicals called endorphins to be released in your brain. Engaging in physical activity helps take your mind off your problems and redirects it to your activity, giving you an awareness of your body in the present moment.

Next time you find your mind starting to race, put your body to work. Turn up some music and move!

I will replace my
negative thoughts
with positive ones

EXHALE

After a long day, or maybe a stressful moment with family, sometimes you just need to breathe. Breathing deeply calms your nervous system, relaxing your mind and body.

Close your eyes and inhale deeply through your nostrils for 3 seconds. Hold your breath for 2 seconds and then exhale through your mouth for 4 seconds. Try not to think of anything while you're doing this except the sound and sensation of your breathing.

Your mind doesn't know the difference between what you do want or don't want. It only knows what you focus on.

Anonymous

GET A GOOD NIGHT'S SLEEP

When you wake up feeling well-rested, it can make a difference to how you feel about the rest of your day. You may believe you're ready take on anything. The benefits of a full night's sleep are many and include increasing your productivity, putting you in a better mood and reducing stress.

Not to mention, after a good night's sleep, you'll be alert and able to appreciate the experiences of the day fully by being in the moment. You should aim for seven or more hours a night to reap the benefits.

I am in charge of
my well-being

STRESS-PROOF YOUR BEDTIME

When we come home after a busy day, it can be hard to unpack the stress and relax, and that can cause restless nights. In a recent survey, 44 percent of adults claimed stress had caused them to lose sleep at least once in the previous month.

Incorporating a bedtime routine will help to let your body know that it's time to wind down for the night. Start by creating a peaceful atmosphere at least an hour before you go to bed. This will help alleviate your stress. Try turning off all electronic screens and avoid participating in any over-stimulating mental activity. Have a cup of tea instead (non-caffeinated of course!) or take a bubble bath. It's been proven that activities like these, which cause your body to switch on its natural relaxation response, improve your sleep by reducing the release of stress hormones like cortisol and adrenaline. This helps your mind and body to calm down.

As you go through the mindful ritual of your bedtime routine, practice focusing on the present. You'll find that there's no room for negative thoughts or worry.

Laughter is important,
not only because it
makes us happy –
it also has actual
health benefits.

And that's because laughter completely engages the body and releases the mind. It connects us to others, and that in itself has a healing effect.

Marlo Thomas

STRIKE A POSE

Downward facing dog, anyone? A daily yoga workout will help reduce stress and increase relaxation, research shows. It's an ancient practice that marries the mind and body through breathing exercises, meditation and poses.

Yoga meets you where you are and keeps you in the present moment. Try simple poses to get started, and be aware of the sensations in your body. Remember, it's important not to push yourself too hard. Notice and accept what is happening to you as you go through the motions without judgment or reaction.

Every man is the builder of
a temple called his body.

Henry David Thoreau

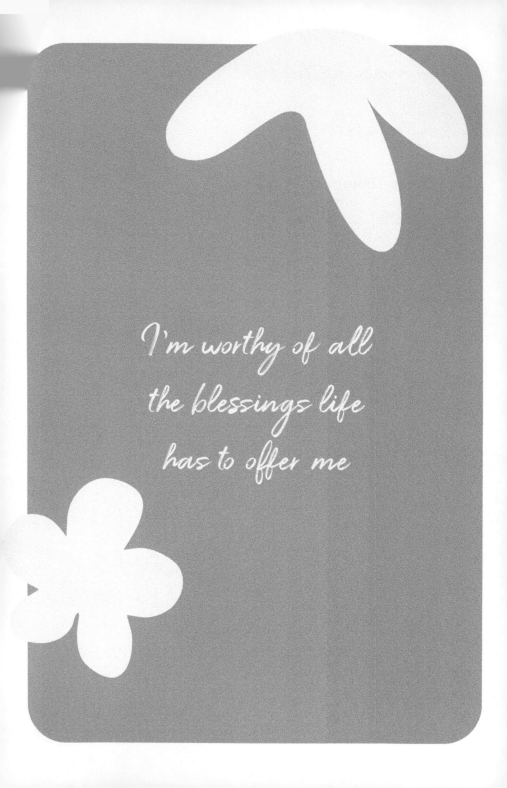

I'm worthy of all
the blessings life
has to offer me

Where there is laughter,
there is no fear. Think about that.
A smile, a simple smile, changes
the chemistry in your body.

Hazel Butterworth

BE CREATIVE

Remember when you were younger and a coloringbook and box of crayons were all you needed to get lost in for a few hours? Research shows that engaging in creative self-expression can boost your mood and alleviate stress and anxiety. Whether writing, singing or dancing is your thing, it all contributes to your overall mind–body wellness. Focusing on creative endeavours helps you concentrate on the activity at hand and keeps you grounded in the present. Explore and experiment, use your imagination – and go create something!

I love taking
care of myself

BE AWARE OF
YOUR BODY

Throughout the day, check in with yourself and do a body scan. Note any sensations you're feeling. Do you have a headache? Are the muscles in the back of your neck tight? Are you tired? Listen to what your body is telling you and see how it is affecting your mood.

You want to stay in tune with your body because stress can be sneaky. It can cause many health issues and you may not realize how serious they are until it's too late. Stress can make you restless and unable to concentrate; in extreme cases, it can be a catalyst for a heart attack. If you want to deal with stress effectively, you need to be aware of the ways your mind and body react to it.

Try to make comparisons between how your body feels during times when you're calm and times when you're under stress, and explore what eases your tension. Engage in activities that will relax your mind, like meditating or sitting outdoors, and you'll find that your body will follow.

I choose to replace my
anxiety with love and
acceptance because
I am worth it

EAT MINDFULLY

Eating healthy foods can directly impact your mood, energy and focus. To get the most out of your meals, practice mindful eating.

Mindful eating means being deliberate about what you put in your body. You'll need to be focused when shopping to ensure that you're purchasing nutritious options to have on hand. Try to make smart, healthy food choices and stick to small portions. When eating, slow down and savor your meal. Take your time and engage all your senses.

Everything you'll ever need to know is within you; the secrets of the universe are imprinted on the cells of your body.

Dan Millman

FIND PEACE
BY YOURSELF

When you need to recharge your batteries, sometimes there's no better way to do it than to seek out alone time. No screens, no distractions: just you and your thoughts. This allows you to give your full attention to the moment and focus on what your mind and body may be telling you. Although it can be intimidating at first, removing all interaction with the outside world can awaken your creativity and provide a respite from sensory overload; focus on your breathing if you feel uncomfortable or overwhelmed. Spend a day getting reacquainted with yourself – you may find a renewed sense of self after having time alone with your thoughts.

I celebrate the connection between my mind and my body

I certainly believe... that nurturing one's spirit is as important as nurturing one's body and mind. We are three-dimensional beings: body, mind, spirit.

Laurence Fishburne

FIND BALANCE

Excess, whether you're working long hours or staying up too late every night, is never a good thing. If you're feeling burned out or tired, your life may be out of balance. Your mind and body are connected, so if you're lacking in one area, the other will also be affected.

Listen to your body. Notice how you're feeling physically and emotionally in the moment. Feeling stressed? Remember, you have the choice to say no to things you don't want to do. Being mindful of your physical and emotional well-being aligns your mind and body to create more harmony in your life.

I accept happiness
and good health
into my life

CHAPTER FOUR

LIVE EVERY DAY

You're probably realizing that to be present, you need to be all in. Why not? You're alive. Whatever else is going on in the world, you're here, right now, which means you have the opportunity to make today your best day. Whatever you're doing, you should make the most of it. Take the moments that life gives you and make them memorable. There are many ways to cultivate joy and wonder, and transform your everyday life into moments where all your senses are alive. Explore how a little spontaneity mixed with mindfulness can help you become more present in your life.

START A MINDFULNESS JOURNAL

There's no better way to practice being present than by keeping a mindfulness journal. Writing about your feelings, good and bad, changes your brain chemistry and helps you deal with feelings and emotions that you may have kept bottled up. Research shows that journaling can increase your sense of gratitude and optimism when you record your positive experiences.

A mindfulness journal also allows you the opportunity to explore what you notice and feel; it's somewhere you can capture what's going on around you without any judgment. There's no right or wrong way to journal: it's your opportunity to write or draw whatever you feel like.

Treat yourself to a notebook and pen or use an app to get started. Try not to censor yourself when you're writing: this is your chance to be honest and share the thoughts you'd probably never say aloud. Make it a daily habit if you can – you'll find it's a great way to reflect on yourself and the world.

LET CURIOSITY LEAD YOU

Have you ever taken a walk and been unsure where it might lead you? Maybe you discovered your new favorite bookshop along the way. When you're curious about the world around you, you'll never cease to be amazed at what you can discover. Researchers have found a link between curiosity and happiness, where one fuels the other, so go lose yourself in exploring something new.

The time to be happy is now;

the place to be happy is here.

Robert G. Ingersoll

BE DARING

Trying new things helps to stretch you mentally, physically and creatively, and hopefully pushes you out of your comfort zone. When you learn a new skill or introduce a new experience, you're asking your brain to think differently. Your creative juices start flowing, and this helps you to stay in the moment because it requires your full attention. Whether you're white-water rafting or singing karaoke in front of a crowd, you need to be all in.

There's also a feeling of accomplishment once you try something new. This helps to relieve stress and triggers the release of endorphins, which keeps you feeling good!

Every day,
I choose to invite
joy into my life

BE KIND

It doesn't take much to do something nice for someone else, and the benefits can certainly outweigh the effort. Practicing kindness and generosity takes the focus off yourself, as you have to be aware of others and their needs in order to perform an act of kindness. It gets you out of your head and helps you develop a sense of connectedness to the moment.

By being fully present, you're able to listen and notice how you can make a difference. Not only are you helping others, but you're also helping yourself. Research shows that when you practice being kind, you increase your empathy, self-esteem and positive emotions.

There are many ways to practice being kind. You can help an older neighbour with tasks, volunteer at a soup kitchen, write a kind letter to a friend - the list is endless. Get started, and you may even inspire someone else to be kind.

The most precious gift
we can offer others
is our presence.

When mindfulness
embraces those we
love, they will bloom
like flowers.

Thích Nhất Hạnh

TAKE A TRIP

Changing your environment, whether it's for a day or a few weeks, encourages you to live in the moment. Being in a new place deepens your powers of observation and heightens your awareness. Wherever you go, always give yourself a few moments to take in and appreciate your surroundings. Being present while observing will help you create vivid memories.

Try to plan a trip where you're able to wander and explore new places in hopes of making wonderful discoveries. When you're flexible and stay open to new experiences, you may find some of your most memorable moments happen quite unexpectedly.

The real question is not
whether life exists after death.
The real question is whether
you are alive before death.

Osho

DISCARD WHAT DOESN'T SERVE YOU

Traditionally, spring marks the time of year when you give your home a deep clean and get rid of items that you no longer use. However, disposing of possessions that clutter your space can be beneficial at any time of the year. You can start by tackling an overrun shelf or take on an entire room. Go through your items and, if you haven't used them in months and don't plan on using them, recycle, donate or get rid of them. It can be liberating when you free up your space and let go of the past. You'll find that you're creating more room to focus on the present.

I observe my environment and find beauty all around me

One of the best things you can do for yourself is to build some regular self-care into your routine - that is, incorporate activities into your day that bring you joy.

You know yourself better than anyone, so only you can figure out what you need to be happy. Try writing a list of activities you find meaningful and that you enjoy, and then schedule the time in your calendar to do them - no rescheduling allowed!

Whatever you choose to do - visit a museum, curl up with a good book, have lunch with friends or try a new activity - to get the most out of your time, be fully present. Don't worry about any emails you need to send or an errand you forgot to run; they'll still be there when you've finished.

Instead, use this time to engage your senses and be in the moment. You'll develop a sense of wonder and awe, which are automatic mood boosters.

FOLLOW YOUR INTUITION

Listening to your inner voice can be a good thing. We're not talking about the inner critic who makes you second-guess yourself. No, intuition is the wise inner voice that comes with being present and knowing yourself. When you are mindful and present, you develop the ability to hear and feel your intuition, which will often lead you to exactly where you need to be.

If you're unsure about a situation, sit still with yourself. Observe what's going on around you and within you. Give space for the quiet voice that's coming from your heart: that's your intuition speaking to you.

Happiness is your nature. It is not wrong to desire it. What is wrong is seeking it outside when it is inside.

Ramana Maharshi

REDUCE YOUR SCREEN TIME

It's no secret that scrolling through social media posts can sometimes make you feel bad. Studies have shown that high usage can increase feelings of loneliness and depression. Give yourself a break by planning an evening or a day without technology. Turn off your screens and focus on real life.

Research shows that reducing your screen time will reduce your stress, improve your focus and help you be more productive. Even if you don't want to go a whole day without your screens, try to limit your use before bedtime – it'll help you sleep better. By paying attention to what's going on around you, you allow yourself to be present for life's moments.

I engage fully with each of my physical senses to experience more joy

FORGIVE AND
MOVE ON

It can be hard to let go of grudges. At some point, everyone has experienced being hurt by the words or actions of another. Sometimes we may even be angry at ourselves for something we did, or should have done. Either way, when you hold on to that resentment, you're not allowing yourself to enjoy the present because your attention is still focused on the past. You have a choice: you can let someone else's actions continue to dictate your mood, or you can move on. To gain a sense of peace, you need to let go of past resentment or anger.

If you're struggling to forgive someone, or yourself, acknowledge your feelings of hurt and accept that people are not perfect. It doesn't make them bad; it makes them human. Try creating a phrase that you can repeat as needed, such as, "I have compassion and empathy, I bear no ill will to anyone," or, "I forgive myself, I deserve love and good fortune."

Once you release your anger, you'll find it much easier to be present for the moments of joy in your life.

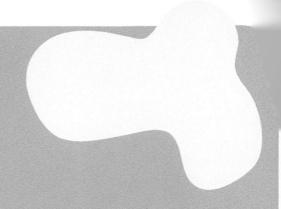

I have the ability to create
the life I've always wanted
by seeking out the wonder
and joy in my experiences

EXPLORE
NATURE

Spending time in nature allows you to cultivate a sense of wonder and appreciation. You don't even have to leave your house – just open a window, feel the fresh air on your face and be aware of the sounds around you.

If you do go outside, researchers find that just being in nature reduces stress. Studies show that people are better able to pay attention in nature, causing their bodies and minds to relax. Practice being present while on a walk in a park or the countryside, using your senses to experience and engage in the moment.

Today I see beauty everywhere I go, in every face I see, in every single soul.

Kevyn Aucoin

SMILE AND THE WORLD SMILES WITH YOU

You don't always have to look outside of yourself to find joy. You have the power to create your own happiness with just a smile.

Studies show that the simple act of smiling can improve your mood and increase your positive thoughts, regardless of why you are smiling. Smiling is also contagious – it's hard not to smile back when you see someone else smiling.

Try it next time you're in a social situation where you feel nervous or unsure. Smile to break the ice and more than likely you'll be greeted with a smile in return. So go on, spread a little joy in your life and others', and share a smile.

*I allow myself
to experience
childlike wonder*

CHANGE YOUR ROUTINE

Having a routine can be awesome, especially if it helps you relax. But sometimes you can find yourself in a rut from doing the same thing, day after day. Maybe you always take the same route to work or buy the same ingredients to make dinner every week. After a while you go through your routine so often, it gets hard to give it your full attention and be in the moment: you could probably do it with a blindfold on. At this point, you may be doing things just to do them, and there's no joy in that.

Research has shown that when you switch up your routine, it can improve your ability to retain information by stimulating the area where we store long-term memories – the hippocampus. This will also help you stay in the moment as you take notice of what you're doing.

So next time you find yourself getting ready to do what you always do, try shaking things up a little. Maybe take a walk instead of eating lunch at your desk, or try cooking something you've never made before for dinner.

Why not just live in the moment, especially if it has a good beat?

Goldie Hawn

FAKE IT 'TIL YOU FEEL IT

Sometimes you're not in the mood to smile. Something happened that threw your whole day off, and you'd rather go somewhere and sulk. It's tempting to wallow in your bad mood, but neuroscience shows that when you go through the motions of being thankful, this will trigger the actual emotion of gratitude in your brain. This will increase your feelings of happiness and help you get in the frame of mind to see a more positive perspective.

You can try giving out compliments, writing a thank you letter or even giving someone a hug. These acts will take you out of your head and help you be in the present moment.

I choose to find
the bright side;
if I want to be
happy, I will be

Whatever the present moment contains, accept it as if you had chosen it. Always work with it, not against it.

Eckhart Tolle

CONCLUSION

Now you see how living in the present helps you experience so much more of your life! Not only that, but hopefully you've also found a renewed appreciation for those around you. Every moment of every day asks us to pay attention, so take the tools that you've gained and practice using them daily. Don't forget the mind/body connection, and let it guide you on your path to a state of calmness and relaxation.

Instead of becoming caught up in the worries about what may or may not happen in the future, be mindful of your experiences as they are happening. Go into each moment with all your senses fully engaged, and hopefully the memories you create will bring you immense happiness and joy every time you recall them.

Remember, this is just one stop on your journey of enlightenment – there's so much to discover!

I am fully present